# A
# Flawed
# Democracy

Cover Design and photography by Elise Grey
www.ladygreycollections.com.au

Objective of this book is

# To Strengthen Democracy

The role of this book is to start serious action toward improving democracy.

It is an attempt to review the basic principles and troubles of the last century in democracy.

Then it is to clarify and redefine the rules under which democracy is administered in a way that ensures that the citizen is the centre of the decision making. That is, the citizen is not just a tool in the functions of capitalism.

This book does not have all the answers but is only a starting platform on which to start debate within the democratic community.

# Table of Contents
## Why Rewrite The Constitution?

## What Needs to be Considered Before Rewriting the Constitution?

- What is the long-term fundamental type of society Australians want to achieve?  What does Australia envisage and strive for in one hundred years, two hundred years...?;
- Government and Religion;
- Further important societal topics (privacy, role of unions);
- The role of the military in domestic situations;
- Accountability and Transparency;
- Behavioural requirements for government and judicial personnel;
- Guidelines for Writing a new Constitutional document;
- What is the model that will be used?

# Why rewrite the constitution?

The constitution is the rule book

for how a democracy is to function.

In Australia it needs to be updated.

# Chapter 1      A FLAWED DEMOCRACY

**"The Parliament shall, subject to this Constitution, have power to make laws for the peace, order, and good government of the Commonwealth with respect to:-**

**(xxvi.) The people of any race, for whom it is deemed necessary to make special laws:[1]"**

A constitution that in 2015 has the above 'race' clause needs an urgent comprehensive rewrite.

In the twenty-first century citizens need to be treated as equals. Any constitution that allows rules to be made by race or religion is not respecting all its citizens and therefore the country's standards of democracy are not adequate.

Yes we can say that various groups are disadvantaged such as the health and life expectancy of Australia's aboriginal population statistically compared with the rest of the nation's population. The average life expectancy of an aboriginal is shorter than the other ethic people in Australia. Likewise, the populations of the coloured people in Australia in jails is out of sync with the proportion of coloured people in society.

This does not mean that there are not whites or other races in a similar situation as the aboriginal. Focus needs to be redefined to

---

[1] http://australianpolitics.com/constitution-aus/text     accessed 23 December 2013

focus on the reasons that are behind this imbalance. Is it financial? Is it historical reasons? Is it the customs and traditions that create the difference? Is it a biological factor? Is it the level of education? What places people of any race in these situations? **To focus on race or religious background causes division**. Again I say that what needs to be done is to focus on a cohesive plan to improve the situation for **all** those citizens who are disadvantaged. Improving the situation for the disadvantaged will help the entire community of the nation. Maybe it's the law enforcement agencies and their officers that need to be educated on management of those in distress and custody?

## The key is to focus on the humanity of goals, processes, rules, laws and policies and to ensure that those implementing and enforcing these are trained appropriately.

To many around the world, and most in Australia, Australia is a land of hope and joy; a lucky country. A land of democracy. It is that, in many cases. But action needs to take place for that to remain into the future.

The twentieth century was a time of change in all spheres, education of the masses, speed and decimation of communication. The society class structure has changed. The middle class grew in size and wealth, radically changing the standards of the society; changing standards for billions of people. Medical care has leapt forward and that can be seen in our increased life expectancy. Racial parameters have changed. In Australia, women gained the right to vote, aboriginals gained the vote, and just like the political sphere in South Africa, everything changed radically. The blacks in America gained equal rights to the whites. In Europe the migration of non-indigenous cultures has radically changed the face of society, and not just in the improvement of food choices and restaurants. Science has become a major religion in the world, leading to less faith in the spiritual realm and dimensions. Travel over land, sea and space has taken on never before conceivable movement of people. Tourism has become a major international industry.

The globally harmonious nature of clothing and education is constantly changing the very nature of cultures, altering cultures that have persisted for centuries largely unchanged.

The many wars of the twentieth century and the associated atrocities (be these the gas used in warfare in the first half of the twentieth century, the Jewish Holocaust in the 1930's and 1940's, the Pol Pot regime in Cambodia, the apartheid practices across the world including, South Africa and the USA, just to name a few of mankind's atrocities of the twentieth century) have changed value systems. The world wars of that century touched all nations on the globe.

The information systems of the twenty-first century mean that local wars now affect all of us around the world with a sense of humanity and fear and varying moral conviction.

Australia may feel a bit smug at this point, but it cannot deny the extermination of many native aboriginal peoples in the years since European arrival only just over 200 years ago. Nor can Australia feel proud about the twentieth century atrocities of the Aboriginal Stolen Generation which lasted for nearly 70 years. In this time the democratic government destroyed the indigenous people's family structures and communities and culture that had stood for thousands of years.

> **Democracy requires rules that do not allow such fracturing of family, communities and generational scarring to occur as the twentieth century did.**

Atrocities cannot be counted purely by the number of dead bodies. Atrocities leave a massive spiritual debt plus moral and community scars that endure for generations.

Add to Australia's sad record in the twentieth century, during the major world war of 1940's, there was the dual atrocity taken by two democratic countries (Australia and Britain) with theses democratic countries working together forcing 160,000 British children to migrate to Australia, with no real concern for their care. This policy was implemented by a moral lie to both parent and child, the lie that the other no longer were alive. The condition in which these children lived and what they endured both physically and psychologically is hard to comprehend by the average person within a democratic nation.

Just as hard to comprehend, is that such policies were happening without the majority of citizens being aware that these actions were taking place.

Plus in Australia in the 1950's-60's and 70's unwed mothers were forced into adopting out their children. Again families and community scars were created and left unhealed. To this day children and parents and extended families are being further harmed by the divorce processes that divide rather than heal and help to move forward in a positive way.

I doubt any democratic nation could honestly say that there have been only good and moral decisions and actions by all arms of its political structure.

Perfection may be hard to achieve but it worth striving for.

A business motivational rhetoric also needs to be the governments: "Working toward excellence is not an option, it is the only option".

Financial power structures are no longer largely geographically based, in national boundaries. This means that the basis of democracy is challenged. A shifting of the authority and control of the fiscal power can be out of the control of government, a government limited by its geographical boundaries. It will take a great degree of intelligence and negotiation to ensure that the focus of a democracy remains focused on what is best for the majority of the country's citizens. With the many international rules being made this is being addressed.

## Democracy is not outdated.

## The constitutional documents are outdated.

The rule books – constitutional documents need to be rewritten before the fundamentals of democracy are lost to a new form of governance where the citizens of the world are subject to the power of commercial enterprises and decisions based on financial issues rather than the best humane outcomes for the majority of the citizens; where elections are no more than a sham of media manipulation and elections come to be just a propaganda exercise for those in control of the media content.

In Australia the government has lost its focus from governance to one of power. The media talk of the parliaments as 'being in power' when it should be more accurately said 'given the authority to control the governance'. Power is too closely associated with control rather than being a servant of the people as it should be for politicians and all public servants.

For example in Australia the rhetoric of the Liberal party while in opposition was always negative and never constructive. Now the Liberal party is in power they continue each day with their political agenda to remain in power. Every speech they make includes the words or statement that says "we are repairing the mess Labor left us". Also included are constant suggestions that the now opposition should be constructive and provide their ideas to the Liberal Party.

And when the Labor leader gives a considered response in parliament, two grossly inappropriate things happened. Firstly the response gained no real media coverage.

Check out the response for yourself:

www.youtube.com/watch?v=Vba36FEoV3E&feature=youtu.be

---

**In Australia the government has lost its focus from governance to one of power**

---

Secondly it is so disrespectful that so few of Liberal Party members are present. This action of non-participation is not only disrespectful to the Labor party but also disrespectful to the citizens of Australia.

So tell me how can citizens make considered responses and decisions when they are only told one side of the story? Need it be asked why much of popular media only gives a skewed picture of the situation?

Likewise in 2014 the Liberal Party is constantly saying that Australia was left in a dire financial situation by the preceding Labor government. They fail to mention that the Labor Party brought

Australia through the Global Financial Crisis with comparatively minimal financial crisis. Nor does the Liberal Party acknowledge that the spending programs that were implemented by Labor were responsible for this and for Australia retaining its triple A financial rating. Nor does the Liberal party acknowledge that Labor had set in place valid plans to address (lower the budget and repay loans) the necessary spending though these years of financial crisis. Politics! When will the citizens be treated with respect and not as mushrooms? How can we change our rule book so citizens can be made the centre of democracy?

New constitutions need to be written to provide clear guidelines for all three wings of government (that currently exist in Australia); these wings being the House of Representatives, the Senate, and the Judiciary

In this book I will be talking about the Australian democracy as that is the one I am most familiar with; and I am more familiar with Australia's culture than any other. Australia's constitution was only written just over a hundred years ago but it is out-dated for the current multicultural society and the changes in values and educational standards that have occurred over the last century.

Australia's constitution was written when it was a colony, when it was part of the political group "The Commonwealth of Nations"; which at a political level no longer exists. This group was headed by Britain; at that time the ultimate decisions for laws and appeals rested with Britain.

All democracies, around the world, are being challenged with the rapid changes, many changes caused by the information access and flow of the twenty-first century. So I hope that much I say here may be worth contemplating for other democratic nations.

The constitution is the rule book of how a democracy will work.

Democracy comes in different forms with each democratic country's working and decisions reflecting its history and culture. None are perfect. I doubt any would ever be perfect.

# Chapter 2

**PROPAGANDA IN DEMOCRACY**

Somehow I found that somewhere in my mind I related serious propaganda only with non-democratic countries. How this thought ever managed to get there must be from false propaganda in a democracy. Due to this misconception of mine, I found it difficult to write this section. The understanding of what has been happening in Australia has shaken my belief in the current form of democracy to my core.

**Australia became a republic in 1986
3 March at 5 a.m.
Greenwich mean time**

I naively had thought that democracy represented openness and honesty, and above all integrity. Sadly, evil can corrupt even the best intentions if not kept in check.

In 2013 around the time of the parliamentary elections, and since they occurred, once again politicians and the media embark on a rhetoric about Australia needing to sever its political ties to Britain and become a republic.

This lie has been brought forward again and again over the last couple decades. What 'lie' you might ask, what is she talking about? Well the fact that:

> The **Australia Act 1986** is the name given to a pair of separate but related pieces of legislation: one an Act of the Commonwealth (i.e. federal) Parliament of Australia, the other an Act of the Parliament of the United Kingdom. While each Act gives its short title as "Australia Act 1986", in Australia they are referred to, respectively, as the Australia Act 1986 (Cth) and the Australia Act 1986 (UK). These nearly identical Acts were passed by the two parliaments, to come into effect simultaneously, because

*of uncertainty as to which of the two parliaments had the ultimate authority to do so.*

*The Australia Act (Cth and UK) eliminated the remaining possibilities for the UK to legislate with effect in Australia, for the UK to be involved in Australian government, and for an appeal from any Australian court to a British court[2]*

The Macquarie Dictionary's definition of a Republic:

*1)A state in which the supreme power rests in the body of citizen entitled to vote and is exercised by representatives chosen directly by them. 2) Any body of persons etc., viewed as a commonwealth. 3) a state, especially a democratic state, in which the head of the government is an elected or nominated president, not a heredity monarch.*

## Australia became a republic in 1986

These Acts are a good thing for Australia, as far as breaking the governmental ties to Britain. However, at this point in 1986 Australia ceased to be based on the Westminster standards from at least two points of view. One is that the British system was based on Christian moral standards and now there are no moral/humane standards. Secondly, with the elimination of the *"possibilities for ... an appeal from any Australian court to a British court"* this removed any accountability for the Australian Judiciary hence Australia from this time created a superior class in the society. The legal profession became exempt from any form of accountability to the citizens of Australia.

Two main political democratic issues arose from the 1986 Australia Acts:

1) It stopped Westminster Parliament and the Queen of England having any power to make any laws or rulings in regard to Australia. The U.S. President or the German Chancellor has as much authority as the Queen of England has in Australia.
2) These acts stopped Judicial Appeals to the British Privy Council. The British Privy Council had been the monitoring system of the judicial decisions within Australia. This leaves Australia's

---

[2] http://en.wikipedia.org/wiki/Australia_Act_1986 retrieved 12 July 2012
Family Law Legislation Amendment (Family Violence and Other Measures) Bill 2011 (Public) Friday, 8 July 2011 Canberra - Emphasis added

Judiciary without any accountability to anyone and completely outside the law. It is definitely not accountable to the citizens of Australia. The judiciary ceased to have the need to be transparent in all its actions, processes and decisions

"So now we must ask ourselves, looking at our constitution and the Australia Act who is in charge?
Who is governing Australia's democracy?

✓ The Judges
✗ Our elected Parliamentary Representatives
✗ Citizens of Australia"[3]

## So from the enactment of the 1986 Australia Acts, Australia became a Republic.

I.    The Queen of England has no political authority in Australia. So retaining the Queen of England as the Queen of Australia clouds Australia's independence. As does retaining the positions Governor General.

II.    The Queen of England's supposed Australian representatives, the governor generals, are political appointments by the ruling party so are just puppets of those parties.

III.    The Governor General's role in governance has no democratic purpose.
So why have the Queen of Australia and the Governor General? Isn't it time to get on with governing and not waste money on a politically irrelevant figurehead half the world away and the roles of Governor General? So is the Queen of Australia for Australia only a bit of expensive decoration on top of other government expenses? Or is the Queen of Australia a screen for citizens to not recognise who truly has power in Australia?

In Australia today less than half the population have British heritage. From the period of WWII, migrants in greater numbers came from other European countries, South America, Asia and Africa. So, the figure head of the Queen of England is not very relevant to most Australians.

---

[3] The Pale Blue Suitcase 2012 page 74

IV.     Many Australians still believe that they can address concerns to the Queen as she has influence of matters of state in Australia. But from the enactment of the Australia Act, Australians cannot make any requests to the Queen Etc. for assistance, as she has no longer had any authority in Australia.

V.     To debate the issue of the British Privy Council for Australia, we (especially Australians) must first understand what this council did:

### Privy Council of the United Kingdom

**Her Majesty's Most Honourable Privy Council**, *usually known simply as the* **Privy Council**, *is a formal body of advisers to the sovereign in the United Kingdom. Its membership is mostly made up of senior politicians who are (or have been) members of either the House of Commons or the House of Lords.*

*The Privy Council,* **the modern-day successor to the Privy Council of England** *and the Privy Council of Scotland, was formerly a powerful institution, but its policy decisions are now exclusively in the hands of one of its committees, the Cabinet. The Council formally advises the Sovereign on the exercise of the Royal Prerogative, and together (as the Queen-in-Council) they issue executive instruments known as Orders in Council, which among other things are used to make Regulations. The Council by itself also has a delegated authority to issue Orders of Council, which are mostly used to regulate certain public institutions. The Council advises the Sovereign on the issuing of Royal Charters, which are used to grant special status to incorporated bodies, and city or borough status to local authorities.*

*Certain judicial functions are also performed by the Queen-in-Council, although in practice the actual work of hearing and deciding upon cases is carried out exclusively by the Judicial Committee of the Privy Council. The Judicial Committee consists of senior judges appointed as Privy Counsellors: Justices of the Supreme Court of the United Kingdom, judges of the Court of Appeal of England and Wales, judges of the Court of Appeal in Northern Ireland, judges of the Inner House of the Court of Session (the supreme civil court in Scotland), and judges from various other Commonwealth member states. The Council was formerly a supreme court of appeal for the entire British Empire (other than for the United Kingdom itself).[4]*

So the removal of the Privy Council from having authority in Australia meant that Australia had a class of people who by obtaining a law degree and progressing up to judicial position are unaccountable to anyone.

As the role of the Judiciary is to interpret laws and make judgments; these functions of the Judiciary, from the enactment of the Australia Act, required neither transparency nor accountability to anyone, particularly to the citizens of Australia.

In being given this "free for whatever option" the judiciary effectively means the judiciary can change the laws made by the voted in representatives. So by default the judiciary became the ruling class of Australia.

The above oversights need to be corrected. The best way to do this in a democracy is by writing a new constitution that is endorsed by the citizens in a referendum.

> "We (the judiciary) believe that ultimately the determination of what goes into legislation is a matter for the parliament.
>
> You are the ones who are accountable to the people, and WE (the judiciary) ARE NOT."[a]

---

[4] http://en.wikipedia.org/wiki/Privy_Council_of_the_United_Kingdom sourced 23 November 2014.

[a] Justice Faulks, Deputy Chief Justice Family Court of Australia Senate Legal and Constitutional Affairs Legislation Committee (emphasis added)

## Chapter 3     THE DEBATE - REPUBLIC OR MONARCHY

In Australia frequently the media is full of the debate: Should Australia be a Republic or a Monarchy?

Just google Australia's Republic debate and you will get hundreds of articles, debates on all forms of media, and blogs.

Just a few that I came up with. There is no particular reason why I chose these others, other than they were the first I came across:

---

*Talks*           *Published 17 July 2014* |
    *IQ2 International Debates*, St. James Ethics Centre

### *The Queen Should be the Last Australian Monarch*

Beyond the declarations of personal admiration for Queen Elizabeth II and the overwhelming lack of affection for politicians of any stripe – the argument is…..
Lining up for the motion is **Marcia Langton**, academic and activist, and **Bob Carr**, former Foreign Minister in the Gillard Government and longest serving Labor premier in New South Wales.
Lining up in support of the *House of Windsor* is **David Aaronovitch**, journalist at *The Times* in London…This *Intelligence Squared* debate, moderated by **Simon Longstaff**, was recorded in collaboration with *BBC Worldwide*.
http://www.abc.net.au/tv/bigideas/stories/2014/07/17/4048371.htm Sourced 13 Aug 2014

---

# Australians have given up on the Republican dream.

## I blame the Duchess of Cambridge

It still boggles the mind that so many Australians seem to not embrace a republican ideal – what arguments are there for our country to remain a constitutional monarchy?

Bridie Jabour      theguardian.com,
Wednesday 29 January 2014 13.49 AEST

http://www.theguardian.com/commentisfree/2014/jan/29/australians-have-given-up-on-the-republican-dream-i-blame-kate-middleton Sourced 13 august 2014

# Republic or monarchy – advance Australia where?

- Saturday, 15 February 2014 16:05
- Written by Matt Doohan

Every once in a while, the long-running monarchy versus republic debate in Australia resurfaces. There are plenty of people supporting either side or many who are not really fussed. I tend to towards the latter. However, I think the issue is well worth discussing…..

http://www.dubbophotonews.com.au/index.php/dpn/categories/opinion-analysis/item/2726-republic-or-monarch-advance-australia-where Sourced August 13 2014

## Chapter 4       POLITICAL PROPOGANDA and POWER

Australia had a referendum in 1999 to address whether Australia should be a republic or continue as a Monarchy. This referendum was misleading as it failed to fully and correctly address the changed situation that the 1986 Australia Act had created.

To me it is clear that although we have had some good (and bad) statesmen over this time, personal power must have played a part in keeping this secret. Other British-Commonwealth countries similarly were given their independence and to different degrees each altered their constitution.

This propaganda alone would be reason for the citizens of Australia to act with wisdom and reclaim their democratic rights to have control of the government by rewriting the constitution. All wings of the government (the Judiciary, the Senate and the House of Representatives) and Australians need to correct this NOW!

Rewrite the whole constitution. No more Band-Aids or minor changes to the preamble. Do the job completely, professionally and keeping focus on the idea that citizens are in control of the country and they want the government to make policies for their best well-being.

Power can become a serious addiction, an addiction that needs to be managed wisely.

To achieve and keep a good democracy means that the members of the House of Representatives, the Senate and the Judiciary need to be transparent and accountable to the citizens of that nation. Politicians need to focus on good governance.

The media need to inform on the acts of parliament. Too often the media reporting on politicians and the legislation is addressed in a similar way to only a seasonal football competition.

This lack of action by the political parties has nothing to do with the party politics. Today we hear Prime Minister Abbot, leader of the Federal Liberal Party, openly state that he is a monarchist. At least he is consistent on this stand. In 1999 Tony Abbott said

*"Republicanism has become a kind of national feel-good pill or constitutional Viagra to be prescribed whether we need it or not."[5]*

Yet there are many in the liberal party who are republicans. Malcolm Turnbull in 1992 eloquently put forward his view:

*"I will be blunt about my prejudices. I am Australian. This is my native land, and I have no other. I believe that Australia's future and prosperity will be greatly advanced if our nation develops a stronger sense of patriotism and national purpose. We need to be prouder of ourselves. We need to love and respect our fellow countrymen much more than we do today, we need to rejoice in those things that make us different and we need to strive to make our nation foremost in every field of endeavour and enterprise. For me, Australia comes first.....We may have a Queen of Australia but we do not have an Australian Queen....Australia undertook the responsibilities of nationhood because it had been turned out by its Mother Country. Our Nationhood was forced on Us. We did not fight for it....The political stability of Australian is a tribute to the political stability of Australians, not the grace and favour of their long-distance monarch."[6]*

All political parties are equally divided in their stance on the situation. My concerns are:

- Why weren't Australians fully informed of the Australia Act and its consequences? Consequences which required revising Australia's constitution.
- I believe the 1999 referendum was inadequate to address the nature of the issue that existed then and still exists.
- The 1999 referendum shouldn't have been just a debate about the monarch vs republic.
- Why didn't politicians and media of the time tell the citizens of the full situation?

I could spend pages trying to work out why the various governments since 1986 kept Australia's citizens in the dark about the Australia Act

---

[5] Page 384 Men and Women of Australia Our Greatest Modern Speeches" by Michael Fullilove Published by Viking (an imprint of Pengui Books Australia)2014
[6] Pages 355 – 362 Ibid

and its implications. I won't do that, as I want to be constructive toward a better Australia and look toward the future.

Australia's national emblem contains a kangaroo and an emu because this animal and this bird can only walk forward. Australians need to get the idea of these symbols and move forward rather than dwell in the past. Start focusing on governance issues.

**Could Many Democratic Nations Have Constitutions That Need Refreshing?**

That depends on the way the constitution was written. Are the rules of government capable of adjusting to the changing times and values? Do they reflect the values of the twenty-first century governance and beyond: including are they capable of manage the changes in power and financial structures. How accountable and transparent are the governing bodies? Is the welfare of the citizen the core of the policies?

# What needs to be considered before rewriting the constitution?

**Chapter 5**                    **A WAY FORWARD**

If a democracy is to provide the freedom, and justice, which it purports to provide, then it must look at the rules in which it operates. I believe a democracy requires rules that do not allow fracturing of family, communities and generational scarring to occur as the past century has. Family fracturing has been evident in a number of government policies of the last hundred years. To name a few, the Stolen Generation of aboriginal Children, ended in the 1970s, The Orange Children around WWII, the forced adoptions of the 1950-60's and currently the exclusion of the Family Law Courts from the Government Inquiry into Paedophilia.

Ultimately the constitution needs to have the approval of its citizens. Before the referendum there needs to be a lot of discussion and consultation, with many to finalise a structure of the governing organisation.
.

In this book I do not pretend I have all the answers on how to write or improve the current constitutions. Nor have I addressed all the issues that need to be updated. I see my comments, concerns and suggestions as a platform for discussion.


**I do not suggest that another form of governance
could be better than fundamental principles of democracy.**
-
**"Government by the people for the people"**

However, we need to be constantly vigilant for the flaws in the rules of our democracies and work on adjusting them. In Australia the rules and the requirements of behaviour for footballers on and off the field have changed and are constantly evolving to meet higher moral and safety standards. Yet the constitution in Australia has not likewise changed. The behaviour of our politicians both in and out of parliament these days means that the footballer has higher behavioural and moral standards to live by than Australian politicians and judges.

**Working toward excellence is not AN option;
it is the ONLY Option**

# Chapter 6      SO WHERE TO START A REWRITE

Until Australians set their goals for their society Australians will constantly have power politics rather than governance.

Factors that need to be clarified before commencing on a constitution:

1) What is the long-term fundamental type of society Australians want to achieve?  What does Australia envisage and strive for in one hundred years, two hundred years...?;
2) Government and Religion;
3) Further important societal topics (privacy, role of unions);
4) The role of the military in domestic situations;
5) Accountability and Transparency;
6) Behavioural requirements for government and judicial personnel;
7) Guidelines for Writing a new Constitutional document;
8) What is the model that will be used?
9) Future Constitution Updates.

## What is the long-term fundamental type of society Australians want to achieve?

No matter what structure is developed for governance I believe that there needs to be a clear outline of the objectives of the constitution. By objectives I mean short and long term goals of what the nation wishes to be now and into the future.

One of these important goals is the preservation and upholding of human dignity. This is important because by setting the standards for acceptable humane conditions, acceptable interaction and privacy will frame the structure for the writing the constitution and acts of parliament, as well as standards for the decisions made by the judiciary in their judgments.

In the past this has been referred to "the rights of an individual".

Democracy's theoretical basis is one of the individual having a say and control in the way the country is run.  Financial issues can be measured in monetary terms such as profit and growth, to name just two. But how do we evaluate "what is best for the individuals".

"Best" so that the citizens are treated with dignity. This balance of dignity and capital power has been witnessed as a battle ground between trade unions and business.

Good economies are important to achieve a good society but this must be balanced so that the individual is looked after and not treated like a commodity for business. Likewise the citizens need to understand this balance and ensure that they work cooperatively with business to achieve a workable balance.

So the broad rights of the individual/level of human dignity needs to be noted in the constitution as a bench mark for the creation of policies and laws and their enforcement.

I believe the United Nations Rights of Individuals and the United Nations Rights of a Child are excellent basis to start from or just use as is (see Appendix).

I was pleased when the House of Representatives and the Senate, under the Prime Ministership of Kevin Rudd, officially adopted these rights into their principles and law making, but annoyed by the way the Judiciary have chosen NOT to accept these as guidelines for their judgements. I appreciate there is a need of the balance of power but on moral principles there needs to be unity between the bodies of governance. Therefore the only way I can see this happen is that these principles are part of the overall constitution.

I see the total list of goals as items that cover how the governing bureaucracy is to provide a society in which:

1. Citizens are able to live in a safe society;
2. All people are treated with respect and dignity;
3. Health care is available to all;
4. Education is provided to all to enable good employment opportunities;
5. Poverty is eliminated (requiring policies for housing and retirement);
6. There are increased living standards for the majority;

7. The nation's natural resources are managed with respect plus the understanding that it is a limited resource that has to be maintained in a viable state for further millenniums;
8. All actions of the governing bureaucracy and the actions of its officers need to be transparent and accountable to its citizens;
9. A humane basis for the decision making in governance;
10. All the wings of governance need to understand that the power is to remain in the hands of the *majority* of the citizens; those people who are given the trusted roles in government need to understand that they are employees of the majority of the citizens;
11. There are opportunities available for all in regard to Freedom of Speech and Freedom of choice of spiritual belief/religion;
12. There are strong provisions for representation in Court.

This is not a bill of rights but overall standards by which all decisions and actions of bureaucracy of governance are striving to build and maintain for its citizens.

## Government and Religion

To separate religion from government is very short sighted, and means that any governance only takes note of part of its true role. The role of governance is to look after the individual and the community welfare. To fail to have faith or look after the soul (the psychological welfare of citizens) will mean that many laws made will fail its citizens and the community's objectives.

All respectable[7] religions acknowledge the soul and caring for others; treating others as you would like them to treat you (even most Atheists abhor evil principles). Respectable religions are based on principals of human welfare and moral standards. To separate the State and Religion will lead to many problems, problems such as depression, many mental illnesses, suicide, use of inappropriate drugs, inappropriate use of alcohol, compulsive gambling (and the list goes on and on).

---

[7] By "Respectable Religions" I mean faiths that encourage harmony, tolerance and caring. I do not include any that may seek to demoralise, are harmful/justify violent practices, intolerant of other respectable faiths, and/or Satanist in their practices.

The financial impact of ignoring the human-soul's needs of citizens will be demonstrated with increased health care costs, suicide and mental health statistics.

As to the issue of a religious organisation as a primary "religion" for a country there should not be one. I believe all respectable faiths need to respect others belief system. This should never be a one way street; nor should education or other government bodies try to homogenise the religions (e.g. stop celebrating Christmas, or ignore Eid al-Fitr, Eid al-Adha). Education should include a curriculum that allows a safe environment learning to understand and respect other respectable faiths.

Faith and Religion has been part of too much of human history to ignore it, nor should we minimize the value it has as a community support group.

## Further Important Societal Topics

1) What rights of privacy is an individual entitled to?
2) What level of privacy is a business entitled to
3) What role do unions have within the community?

## The role of the military in a domestic situation

Daily on the news we see many articles about injustices in war-torn countries as well as countries that consider themselves a good democracy. As I read and watch the many situations, I see that the instability in most areas is based on the use of money and/or military to control citizens in many nations. The actions of those in governance need to be directed toward decisions and actions that are based on human decency, and a focus on the needs of the majority.

New constitutions need to be written to take into account the use of the military in internal matters of a nation.

## Accountability and Transparency

What **transparency and accountability** should all the wings (Judiciary, Senate, House of Representatives etc.) of governance have to the citizens of Australia?

1) How will the government departments be held responsible;
2) Transparency of political fundraising;
3) How will the salary of politicians, judiciary etc. be set and altered

4) Should we have a two party system or one that puts more emphasis on individual representation?
5) Should elections be at set dates?
6) Should the voting be first past the post or preferential voting or some other system? What is the most accurate representation of the citizens? Australia's senate voting ballot papers may be viewed as doubtful representation especially when using the preferential voting system and the party system.

This list keeps on going and could take pages and pages. Best to get the community at all levels involved in the discussion.

## Behavioural Expectations of Members of The Houses of Parliament and The Judiciary

The constitution needs not only the rules of government and the humanitarian/dignity standards of the society but also needs to clearly define society's behavioural expectations of members of the houses of parliament and the judiciary. Clarifying these here is necessary to provide a complete operation for governance.

**Whatever model is used there are standards that will need to be stated:**

**1)** Behavioural
**2)** Honesty/Integrity[8]
**3)** Disclosure
**4)** Primary focus is representation of constituents.

---

[8] This will include items such as pecuniary interests, appropriate use of funding and correct procedure for granting of government contracts etc..

Considerations for Proposed Standards of

# BEHAVIOUR & OTHER REQUIREMENTS
### For All Representatives
### Of Both the Houses of Parliament and Judiciary

1. The power given to politicians, judges and senior government officers can often bring people into these jobs who are quite charming and personable people, but who may have personal interests outside of those of their constituents. So to ensure the integrity of their person involvement all these groups (Member of the Senate, Members of the House of Representatives and Members of the Judiciary –who will be referred to as "Senior Officials") must be transparent as to their financial interests and other relevant involvements which could impact on their impartial decision making.

2. Secondly these senior officials must realise their behaviour is a role model to all citizens; therefore their actions must be of a mature and high moral standard, including their ability to be both empathetic and genuinely sympathetic.

   Abusive language or bullying actions are not constructive or appropriate, nor acceptable. Such senior representatives of the nation should be warned and even removed (and replaced) from their positions if they cannot provide dignity to their representative or judicial roles.

3. Wage increases for both politicians and judges must be linked with the increases in pension payments and the minimum wage. As the increase usually is a percentage figure then the increase in government incomes needs to be half of that given to pensions. (I choose half to counter the huge inequality between pensions of every day citizens and the lifetime pensions of politicians and judges) If the judiciary and parliament grant themselves a wage increase of 4% then they must at the same time provide an 8% increase to pensioners and the basic hourly rate for workers.

   Check out this article on judges/magistrate salaries over 2012 & 2013:

   http://www.canberratimes.com.au/act-news/magistrates-call-for-pay-rise-20131016-2vn6b.html

*'The salaries of judges recently rose from $402,880 to $412,550. Using the 80 per cent benchmark, magistrates' salaries would climb from $290,958 to $330,040*

*Canberra's magistrates are seeking a $39,000 pay rise, while the Master of the ACT Supreme Court wants a new formula to determine his salary which would deliver him an extra $29,000 next year.'*

In Australia a pensioner gets about $400 a week, that's around $20,000 per year to live on after a lifetime of work and paying taxes. You must agree that there is an imbalance of principles when you look at the welfare cuts that were being made over the same period of time as the increases for the judiciary.

The politician, judge, public servant and the pensioner is paid out of the same purse (government income/taxes etc.). Therefore it is reasonable to assume that if politicians and judges can get pay increases that also should pensioners. At the same time the equity of retirement funds should at the same time implement laws that counteract impoverishing citizens on the pension and increasing financial difference between the pensioner and the public servant/politician/judge.

So should there be a statement in the constitution that enables that with any increase in income or benefits of the voted in members that a proportionally appropriate increase is given to all public servants, pensioners and increase to the minimum wage rate?

## Principles when making a law or ruling

4.  All rulings, judgments, laws, acts of parliament are to support the principles of dignity of the individual and child that is adopted by the constitution
5.  'When making a law, there needs to be clearly defined objectives and desired outcomes that are the basis for the need to have, or change, the law. That is, laws need to have objectives and outcomes that can be measured; that are automatically measured from the time the law is implemented, and then, at least annually, reported on to demonstrate the success of these objectives. These

are the key performance indicators (KPI) for the law. If the law does not achieve these objectives; then there is the need to review the law and the processes. In doing so, find out if it is the law or its implementation and interpretation that are at fault or other; and then adjust what needs to be adjusted to meet the laws KPI. These KPI need to be part of the publication processes'[9].

6. Every clause in the new constitution needs to first clarify the reason and purpose of the clause. This would enable a better understanding of the constitution and enable easier interpretation of the constitution. Plus this would give a standard to evaluate whether the clause continues to have relevance to the changing community standards.

7. All judges must note the desired outcomes from their rulings and follow up the consequences of their rulings in a process to improve the desired outcomes of their rulings.

8. All judgements, desired outcomes, and reasons for judgements are to be published (as for laws noted above) so that citizens can monitor the implementation of the laws. The identity of judges is to be published; the names of <u>convicted</u> criminals can be published; however the other people involved in the matter will NOT have their identity exposed especially in child and family matters nor the identity of victims of crime without the victims' permission.

---

[9] Page 74 *The Pale Blue Suitcase* by J.Ehrlich 2012

## Guidelines for Writing a New Constitutional Document

1.  What style of language should be used?
    On this point I think the language should be that of the average educated adult Citizen can understand.
    Definitely not the use of Legalise, as that would need interpretation for the majority of citizens.
2.  What language should it be written in? English
3.  What format should the document be written in?

## What is the Model that will be used?

To set the rules of governance the first thing is to decide the structure of the government. Is Australia to follow and replicate other systems that exist? That of England, USA, Germany, China, New Zealand, Canada, South Africa, Greece...? Or use these models for ideas and build a unique governing structure, a structure that best suits the Australia of today and Australia's hopes for the future.

The fact is Australia is a republic. A model needs to best suit Australia's multiculturalism and multi-religious/spiritual beliefs. The challenge is to create a model that encapsulates the Australian Spirit and principles of caring for each other. This requires clear guidelines balancing the individual human rights of dignity and goals of society as a

> **All wings of governance need to understand that the power is to remain in the hands of the majority of the citizens.**

whole. In sports teams each individual needs to be themselves and at the same time play to achieve the goals of the group. In sport this is to win. But in a social context what does the Australian Community want to achieve?

Please do not think that I dislike Queen Elizabeth II and her family. I admire them greatly and think they are a great part of Australia's history. And their presence in today's world is wonderful. Wonderful in that they provide people of good a value system. A value system that generally is far better than the fleeting role models provided by many 'famous' celebrities. I hope the monarchs of this world (be they England or Denmark or...) continue for centuries to provide a standard that can be admired.

But the Australia Acts of 1986 made the choice of a republic or monarch irrelevant.[10]

> *"It is only since 1986 that an ultimate court of appeal ceased to be a tribunal of English judges, the Privy Council, sitting in London....Societies which have turned their back on social or political progress have invariably atrophied and collapsed."*
>
> Malcom Turnbull[11]

(See chapter 10and 11 for specific suggestions)

## Future Constitution Updates

With the rapid changes that are happening in development human communities and communication, should the constitution enable the document to be revised as humanity and knowledge improves?

1. If yes, then what are the rules regarding how to make a change?
2. Should there be regular constitution reviews every 50 years? If yes how will this work?
3. How will it be funded?
4. How will the average citizen be involved in this process?
5. Should there be regular official reviews that make recommendations that are accepted or rejected in a referendum?

---

[10] I wonder how much of a budget saving it would be to not have the expenses involved with the monarch system Australia has. Turning buildings such as Government House and Kirribilli house into venues for the public of Australia could help balance the budget.
[11] Ibid

# Chapter 7    GLOBAL CORPORATIONS

Another large change in the world that has affected all countries is the impact of large multinational corporations. These corporations have created many wonders for all the citizens of the world. Yet just as they are not bound by geographical boundaries, they are not bound by the will of the people. Consequently the core principle of democracy is out of balance. Multinational corporations sway citizens of the world with the blurring of borders, cultures and traditions.

> **On a global basis how can the multinational corporation and democracy develop together with human dignity as the core of their actions?**

In past centuries, generally, the income of nations was bigger than that of corporations. Today some corporations' wealth often intimidates that of many nations. The influence of individual nations to govern has become difficult. Yes the United Nations organization is trying to address this among many other issues.

The impact of multinational corporations is extensive for the individual citizen. As the income of corporations can be moved between nations the corporations avoid tax in the countries they choose; this places a greater burden on the individual income tax payer to fund the plans the country want/needs. Likewise the multinational can move operations between countries so that individual jobs can be lost from one country to another country to where conditions provide a more profitable corporate outcome. Hence the wooing of multinational's operations by politicians is a key part of governments fund raising activities.

I am not suggesting that corporations are bad or evil force. There are many great and good things that have come with the growth of global corporations and many inappropriate things as well. The twentieth century produced some amazingly great corporations that managed to have great success while showing wonderful human caring and understanding for its employees and their communities, as well as providing aid to communities/countries in need.

On a global basis how can the multinational corporation and democracy develop together with human dignity as the core of their actions?

Good economies are important to achieve a good society but this must be balanced so that the individual is looked after and not treated like a commodity for businesses/corporations/industries.

Likewise citizens need to understand this balance and ensure that they work cooperatively with business to achieve a workable balance for business. Corporations and shareholders need to be cognitive of the balance required between profit and the society's welfare.

**On a global basis
How can the
multinational
corporation
and
democracy
develop together
with human dignity as
the core of their actions?**

# Chapter 8                    TRADE UNIONS

Many governments in Australia have based their style of fiscal policy on one that counters the power of the union movements, in the belief that unions are not interested in the growth of business and the GDP. This places corporations at odds with the union movement, involving these business structures (corporations and unions) in a quarrel or at war with each other.

What the government should be is arbitrator to obtain the best for its citizens, citizens who are often both a member of unions and corporations.

In the bigger picture how does a nation ensure that the development of corporations and unions and people is done ethically and in the best interests of its citizens in their geographical area of governance?

What is the role of the Workers Union in the political environment?

Will this change if the two party system changes?

Should the role and rights of unions be noted in the constitution? I know that unions have been vital in giving the average citizen the ability to negotiate better human standards in the workplace.

Political parties who fight against unions may hold a prejudice against a section of the citizenship base. Is that ethical? Is this prejudice taking the best interest of the citizens into account?

A union is no more than an interest group that works for the improvement of a situation. Just as there are movements/groups that fight against issues such as saving the Great Barrier Reef.

Should there be rules for these interest/welfare groups in the way they operate? I think there should be but only for the prevention of corruption of the use of the members' funds and welfare.

What the government should be is
arbitrator
to obtain the best
for its citizens;
citizens who are often both
a member of unions and corporations.

# Chapter 9

## THE HOUSE OF REPRESENTATIVES, THE SENATE & SUPPLY

The current way for voting in these two wings of governance is appropriate.

## THE HOUSE OF REPRESENTATIVES

The House of Representatives as equal representation of the citizens appears to work adequately.

However I think that the term of government should be a fixed date so focus is on governing not "when is the best time for the next election?" Not one run by the media with the –"what are the polls currently saying" as the factor for date of the next election.

## THE SENATE

The makeup of the Senate, giving equal representation for each state, provides a good balance that will take in the overview of what is best for Australia as a whole. To have equal representation for this Senate would lead to the situation that the state with the largest population would have control of the country and the needs of the less populous state would become an ignored factor.

But the way of voting that is first passed the post or preferential counting or some other method needs to be revisited.

The nature of a warlike style of government and placement in the seating and office arrangement of the members of the Senate and House of Representatives needs to be considered. More on this is mentioned in Chapter 11.

## SUPPLY

Supply has become a major issue since the Labor Government under Gough Whitlam was sacked by the Governor General; subsequently a new election was held. The reason for this was that the budget that was put forward by the Labor party was not passed by the Senate. The election of the senate and the date of change of power of the members of the Senate do not always correlate with the election for the House of Representatives. So this alone can mean that at times, the majority party in House of Representatives may not be the same as that of the

Senate. This may be another good balance of power and safety check for the citizens.

But blocking supply has a major impact on the country as this stops payment for wages for government workers and services are restricted. These vital services include hospitals, ambulance services, fire Brigades, Medicare, roads and other ongoing construction work and some utilities.

The upheaval caused both by blocking the budget and "instant" new elections is counter-productive for the smooth operation of the country. So a clear pragmatic way to keep the society operating needs to be put into the constitution.

A simple way to overcome this problem is to split the budget into

A)  Unchanged items which includes the continuance of the everyday operations of all government departments and authorities.

B)  Independently list the changes to the budget and put each of these up to the Houses of Parliament separately for discussion and approval or not.

So the items in A above are not contested items and therefore the running of the country can continue to operate.

The items in B then come into force within a week or nominated date after approval; the effect of these changes cannot be backdated.

**Transparency of government expenditure** also needs to be closely monitored and reported to the citizens on a regular basis, say monthly. A monthly balance sheet needs to be made available for viewing with operational expenditure of all departments (including the parliaments and politicians expenditures) and comparisons to planned costings on a monthly basis not just something that is brought up each election as an issue for throwing mud at the other party. These reports should be made on-line. An educated population needs to be given this information so informed citizens can raise concerns when they arise.

# Chapter 10          THE JUDICIARY

"We (the judiciary)
believe that ultimately the determination of what goes into
legislation is a matter for the parliament.
You are the ones who are accountable to the people, and
WE (the judiciary) ARE NOT."[12]

It is judges who are the ones who ultimately decide what legislation means and if laws are constitutional; as well as how to interpret and implement laws/legislation.

And the judiciary's decisions are not accountable to the citizens who pay their salaries. This is not right. This is not democracy.

## SEPARATION OF  POWER

I agree there must be a separation of powers and decision making between the Judiciary and the Houses of Parliament.

Although it is assumed that all the branches under the separation of powers do not overlap, there is sometimes a 'common ground' between all three levels.

But where is that separation a good thing and where would this safety barrier be harmful/detrimental to democratic society?

> The doctrine of the **separation of powers in Australia** divides the institutions of government into three branches: legislative, executive and judicial. The legislature makes the laws; the executive put the laws into operation; and the judiciary interprets the laws. The doctrine of the separation of powers is often assumed to be one of the cornerstones of fair government. A strict separation of powers is not always evident in Australia; instead the Australian version of separation of powers combines the basic democratic concepts

---

[12] Justice Faulks, Deputy Chief Justice Family Court of Australia Senate Legal and Constitutional Affairs Legislation Committee
Family Law Legislation Amendment (Family Violence and Other Measures) Bill 2011 (Public) Friday, 8 July 2011 Canberra –( Emphasis added)

embedded in the Westminster system, the doctrine of "responsible government" and the United States version of the separation of powers. The issue of separation of powers in Australia has been a contentious one and continues to raise questions about where power lies in the Australian political system.[13]

Doctrine that enables laws made by the parliament to be interpreted in a way that was not intended by parliament and out of line of the wishes of the majority of citizens needs to be addressed. As should all doctrine within parliament and judiciary.

Judgements and sentencing could be out-of-line with the issues that a law was enacted by the houses of parliament to safeguard. Frequently we hear of family court orders that enable an abusive parent to care for their children, often leaving the children in, at least, a psychologically unsafe situation; or evidence is disregarded leading to problematic judgments enabling paedophiles to gain primary or sole custody.

## ACCOUNTABILITY

Accountability is extremely important at all levels of government.

Accountability is vital to the core of democracy.

Transparency also is what democracy is about.

Judgements on legislation/laws also need to have the same level of responsibility to citizens.

The citizens of the nation should know

1) Exactly where their money is being spent.
2) The plans of future acts of parliament prior to the item being presented to government, so the citizens can have their opinions heard prior to implementation.
3) The objective for all acts of parliament, and subsequently what the outcome of the act does.

---

[13] http://en.wikipedia.org/wiki/Separation_of_powers_in_Australia sourced Nov. 2014

Currently the Australian government keeps using the excuse of security not to divulge the actions and outcomes of the refugee policies it has put in place. Many citizens question the validity of this, especially when looking at the welfare of refugees in government care on Australian land or at off-shore processing centres that have been negotiated with other countries.

'I believe that the power needs to be put back into the hands of citizens of Australia. So how do we go about achieving this correct form of governance?

> A. When making a law, there needs to be clearly defined objectives and outcomes that are the basis for the need to make, or change, the law. That is, laws need to have objectives and outcomes that can be measured; that are automatically measured from the time the law is implemented, and then at least annually reported on to demonstrate the success of these objectives. These are the key performance indicators (KPI) for the law. If the law does not achieve these, then look into it and find out if it is the law or its implementation and interpretation that are at fault; and then adjust what needs to be adjusted to meet the law's KPI.
>
> B. Set all judicial positions with term limits and KPIs: subsequently remove judges who are not up to standard.
>
> C. Vote in the senior judiciary with term limits similar to the Representatives in the Senate. Ensure that each state and the territories have a judge-representative'[14]

---

[14] The Pale Blue Suitcase Divorce Pathways by J Ehrlich published 2012 pages 75 -78

**PRECEDENT** is another stumbling block in the current system in Australia.

Precedent is another stumbling block in the current democratic system in Australia

Precedent is the use of the judiciary to rely on past judgements to make current judgements. A precedent is a decision made previously in courts under different or old laws; in many cases, by the use of precedent, new laws can be ignored. The use of precedent can make laws, made by the voted-in parliamentary representatives, null and void.

If any nation is to move forward from its past mistakes, toward improved-humane decisions and systems, than it needs to ensure that precedent of prior cases is not relevant in making judicial judgments. Instead judicial decisions need to focus on the relevance and correctness of the law in regard to the humane/moral value system and principles set out in the constitution.

Who would consider the decisions made under Hitler's rule as good precedents? Or who would consider the Aboriginal Stolen Generation rulings as good precedents? Hopefully, no good person would. So the constitution of a country needs to ensure that the possibility of using precedent is not available to the judiciary in monitoring and applying laws made by the other wings of governance.

During the time from 1986 to present (2015 and until a new constitution is accepted) Australia has and is effectively a regime with the majority party creating alliances with the judiciary; alliances which mean that Australia is not a democracy. The ultimate power has been in the hands of the judiciary, a judiciary that is not accountable to the people, nor accountable to anything. This means Australians need to restructure their government and rewrite their constitution to meet those changes.[15]

---

[15] As I go through my suggestions for change I may sound as if I am very negative about the judiciary and legal profession in Australia. I am, due to my experiences which I wrote about in *"A Lioness from Judea Roars – A Lioness from Judea Cries".*[15] Please read this if you are seriously interested in understanding my attitude toward this professional sector.

**Extract from The Pale Blue Suitcase Divorce Pathways   pages 78-82:**

## "VOTING IN THE JUDICIARY

Accountability is expected for any area of our modern society except for the judiciary. These public servants are not, by way of Australia's constitution, accountable to anyone. I would not dream of suggesting that all levels of the judiciary need to be elected. To suggest this is equivalent to having the entire body of public service managers voted in. We depend on our politicians to keep these in check. Likewise in the private sector public corporations vote in the Board of Directors not all the employees at management or other levels.

I believe the High Court Judiciary needs to be voted in by the citizens of Australia. These employees of the people then need to have a fixed term in which they ensure laws enacted in the houses of parliament are implemented in line with the wishes of the citizens of Australia.

Let's look first at what is the current situation.

### The High Court

*There have been twelve Chief Justices and 42 Justices since the Court was established in 1903, including the current members of the Court. Three members of the Court – Sir Isaac Isaacs, Sir Ninian Stephen and Sir William Deane – resigned from the Court to become Governor-General. The current Justices of the High Court and the dates they were sworn in, are as follows:*

- *Chief Justice French AC, 1 September 2008*
- *Justice Gummow AC, 21 April 1995*
- *Justice Hayne AC, 22 September 1997*
- *Justice Heydon AC, 11 February 2003*
- *Justice Crennan AC, 8 November 2005*
- *Justice Kiefel, 3 September 2007*
- *Justice Bell, 3 February 2009*

*Appointment*

*Under section 72 of the Constitution, Justices of the High Court:*

- o *Are appointed by the Governor-General in Council;*
- o *Cannot be removed except by the Governor-General in Council on an address from both Houses of Parliament in the same session, praying for such removal on the grounds of proved misbehaviour or incapacity;*

- o *Receive such remuneration as the Parliament may fix; but the remuneration shall not be diminished during their continuance in office; and*
- o *Must retire on attaining the age of 70 years.*[16]

The **High Court of Australia** *is the supreme court in the Australian court hierarchy and the final court of appeal in Australia. It has both original and appellate jurisdiction, has the power of judicial review over laws passed by the Parliament of Australia and the parliaments of the States, and interprets the Constitution of Australia. The High Court is mandated by section 71 of the Constitution, which vests in it the judicial power of the Commonwealth of Australia. The High Court was constituted by the Judiciary Act 1903.*[17]

On 21 August 2012, Attorney-General Nicola Roxon announced that Stephen Gageler, the Solicitor-General, would replace Gummow on the court in October.[18]

**Current Justices of the Australian High Court**[19]

| Name | State | Date Appointed | Retirement | Years* |
|---|---|---|---|---|
| Chief Justice Robert French | WA | 2008 | 2017 | 9 |
| Justice William Gummow | NSW | 1995 | Oct 2012 | 17 |
| Justice Kenneth Hayne | VIC | 1997 | 2015 | 15 |
| Justice Dyson Heydon | NSW | 2003 | 2013 | 10 |
| Justice Susan Crennan | VIC | 2005 | 2015 | 10 |
| Justice Susan Kiefel | QLD | 2007 | 2024 | 17 |
| Justice Virginia Bell | NSW | 2009 | 2021 | 12 |
| Justice Stephen Gageler | ACT | Oct 2012 | 2028 | 16 |

*This last column is the number of years these judges will have the secure position to rule on all decisions made in Parliament.

This means that these individuals are the most powerful people in Australia, yet they are not accountable to anyone. So this power in the hands of a few unelected public servants puts forward the question:

---

[16] High Court of Australia, "About the Justices." Retrieved 18 October 2011 from http://www.hcourt.gov.au/justices/about-the-justices (emphasis added)

[17] High Court of Australia." Retrieved 18 October 2011 from Wikipedia, http://en.wikipedia.org/wiki/High_Court_of_Australia

[18] Retrieved 30 August 2012 From Wikipedia http://en.wikipedia.org/wiki/List_of_Justices_of_the_High_Court_of_Australia

[19]ibid.

"Is Australia a true democracy?"

Note above underlined, *removal on the grounds of proved misbehaviour or incapacity*. These are the only grounds for removal from these positions.

There are no qualifications for them to be responsible in their judgments or have these judgements in line with the wishes of the citizens of Australia. (Nor are the judiciary required to abide by any of the United Nations human rights agreements made by our politicians due to the division of power)

Why should these judges be accountable? Look at a couple of cases in history. Since 1903 Australia has a horrendous record of looking after the welfare of children and mothers. Looking, just at the big issues, lets firstly consider the Stolen Generation from the Aboriginal nations of Australia, the removal of Aboriginal children continued until the mid-1970s; then look at the forced immigration of 160,000 children from Britain that lasted from 1950's to the 1970's. Both have received apologies from the government in recent years.

Kevin Rudd made an apology to the Stolen Generation of the Aboriginal people. His speech included:

> *The nation is demanding of its political leadership to take us forward. Decency, human decency, universal human decency, demands that the nation now steps forward to right a historical wrong... Indigenous children were forcibly taken from their mothers and fathers. That, as a result, up to 50,000 children were forcibly taken from their families. That this was the product of the deliberate, calculated policies of the state as reflected in the explicit powers given to them under statute...* "[20]

As Kevin Rudd said "*The nation is demanding of its political leadership to take us forward decency, human decency, universal human decency, demands that the nation now steps forward to right a historical wrong.*"[21] Then need the Judiciary (which is part and parcel of the political leadership in Australia's

[20] Rudd, Kevin. "Apology to Australia's Indigenous Peoples." Retrieved 18 February 2012 http://australia.gov.au/about-australia/our-country/our-people/apology-to-australias-indigenous-peoples
[21] Ibid

constitution), needs the Judiciary are made accountable to the people of Australia.

So how do we go about making the judiciary accountable? My suggestion is that the High Court judges need to be elected by the citizens of Australia just like we vote in our senators; to do this we need to change the constitution, and this can only be done by a referendum.

## Chapter 11     SUGGESTED STRUCTURE
## of the GOVERNING AUTHORITIES

### Oppositional Basis of Parliament

The oppositional basis of parliament is one based on warlike nature rather than cooperative and constructive governance. The historic basis of this can be understood with the dynamics of the time that the constitution of many nations was developed. This two party formula in this day and age is counter-productive and does not take into account the changed nature of populations. It has the tendency for the individual representative to hold two different alliances, one to his or her constituents and the other to his/her party alliance.

An authentic democracy should be one where the alliance of the voted-in representative is to their constituents rather than to his/her party.

Therefore I believe that we need to develop on a system that encourages individual representatives to conscience vote with a view to his/her electorate's benefit rather than vote on party lines.

Alliances will always exist and the nature of compromise often is necessary. But to focus on the party first is not beneficial.

**Architecture in Parliament**. The very way that voted in members are seated in Australia's parliament is war-like and oppositional. Changing this could alter the behaviour in Parliament. It might be worth considering having members seated according to the alphabetical list of their electoral seat names. Likewise at parliament house the location of the office for each electorate should be allocated by electoral seat names. The office location should remain unchanged following an election.

### Prime Minister Selection
Also the Leader of the country/the Prime Minister should not necessarily the simply be leader of the party with the largest representation in the House of Representatives.

Taking note of all the above leads me to suggest the following structural/organisational changes.

# Structure of the Governing Authorities

Australia has based its structure around the three arms of the House of Representatives, the Senate and the Judiciary, with a fall back on the Governor General (as representative of the Queen of England). This is inappropriate as the Queen of England has not been involved with Australia's governance since 1986.

My suggested **FUTURE STRUCTURE FOR AUSTRALIA** is:

a) Electors should vote in representatives for The House of Representative as proportional representatives

b) Electors should vote for the members of The Senate in the same representation as currently stands.

c) Electors should vote in High Court Judges with fixed terms as that for the members of the Senate. Alternatively the judges could be voted in on fixed five year terms. As there are seven High Court judges I recommend that each state have one High Court Judge to represent each state and a seventh to represent the territories jointly. (As mentioned in Chapter 7)

d) All terms of office for the House of Representatives are set regular terms, with dates nominated in the constitution. (e.g. The last Saturday in May every 4 years) therefore preventing election timing to be run by media polls. These set terms are applicable to the House of Representatives, Senate and voted in Judiciary. (I believe all judges positions should be a fixed term of 5 years, at which time it will be open for review and possible retention by popular vote or open to other candidates by a new vote.)

e) Members of the Senate and member4s of the House of Representative should hold a joint meeting within a week after the election. At this joint sitting they nominate and vote one of their members (from either House (Senate or Representatives) as the Prime Minister of Australia. Nomination and voting may need to take place over a couple hearings but should occur within the first week after an election.

f) If the prime minister is part of the House of Representatives then Senate members nominate-vote in their senior representative. Or if the Prime Minister is a member of the Senate then the House of Representatives vote in their senior representative.

g) The voted in High Court judges nominate who will be their senior representative.

h) These three senior representatives will form the 'Senior Representative Committee of the Government' for emergency decisions. This Committee will cooperatively and jointly take on the responsibilities that previously have been those of the Governor General.

## Protocols of Parliament House

These are many and complex:
http://www.dfat.gov.au/protocol/Protocol_Guidelines/15.html
Many protocols relate back to a different time in history and are not appropriate for this day and age, no more than an antique car would be best for today's roads.

With a rewrite of the constitution these protocols need to be reviewed and written down and accepted as part of the constitution.

Protocols should be

1. Constructive

2. Efficient

3. Effective in getting the business of governance done
   An effective government would plan to act as the board of a major multinational company and at all times be professional in its activities.

4. Respectful to the Citizens of Australia.

If we place the major importance of a voted in member on representing his/her constituents then I wonder if protocols such as making the speaker of the House of Representatives a voted in parliamentary representative is inappropriate. Possibly the speaker's role could be a nominated senior member(s) of the Judiciary, but not a voted in member of the judiciary, possibly on a rotational basis.

## Media Polls

Elections are there to vote in senior public servants who are working for the people and assessed on their achievements in office. Elections are a performance assessment by the citizens of the politician over the whole political term.

The use of polls by the media is a meaningless and largely useless tool as it marks popularity. Polls turn politics in a sports match where they work on the current result from one or a few games of a season, not the overall result of the whole season and the grand-final. Media political polls lower the level of democracy in vision and achievements to a nonsensical level of stupidity.

## Chapter 12   TAKING A LOOK at the CONSTITUTION

### Don't throw the baby out with the dirty bathwater!

Yes there are things that worked in the last constitution, so we need to look at each section and keep the purpose of it, if it is valid for 21st century ( and beyond).

Also there is a level of nonsense in number of existing sections these need to be lost.

Below is a small extract from Australia Constitution as it was in 2014.

Overall:

- The language needs to be changed to language standard that can be understood by the average English speaking citizen. (Many sections I don't have a clue what it is about and English is my first and only language and I am tertiary qualified). The language standard alterations should be done by a suitably qualified academic.
- Many words need to be replaced such as "a writ" to "a formal written order" or something easier to understand.
- Should the "Commonwealth of Australia" be replaced with the "Nation of Australia" or should it just be "Australia"
- Every paragraph requires the objective and purpose for it being part of the constitution.

**Australia's Constitution as 2014**[22]

Australian Constitution – Preamble

The Australian Constitution is contained in an Act of the British Parliament. This is because the British Parliament was the only body in 1900 which could make laws for the whole of Australia; the parliaments of the various colonies, as they then law made by the British Parliament was the only legal way to establish a system of government for the whole of Australia. The act is entitled:

**COMMONWEALTH OF AUSTRALIA CONSTITUTION ACT**

An Act to constitute the Commonwealth of Australia

[9th July 1900]

Whereas the people of New South Wales, Victoria, South Australia, Queensland, and Tasmania, humbly relying on the blessing of Almighty God, have agreed to unite in one indissoluble Federal Commonwealth under the Crown of the United Kingdom of Great Britain and Ireland, and under the Constitution hereby established:

And whereas it is expedient to provide for the admission into the Commonwealth of other Australasian Colonies and possessions of the Queen:

---

[22]http://australianpolitics.com/constitution-aus/text

Be it therefore enacted by the Queen's most Excellent Majesty, by and with the advice and consent of the Lords Spiritual and Temporal, and Commons, in this present Parliament assembled, and by the authority of the same, as follows:-

1. This Act may be cited as the Commonwealth of Australia Constitution Act.
2. The provisions of this Act referring to the Queen shall extend to Her Majesty's heirs and successors in the sovereignty of the United Kingdom.
3. It shall be lawful for the Queen, with the advice of the Privy Council, to declare by proclamation that, on and after a day therein appointed, not being later that one year after the passing of this Act, the people of New South Wales, Victoria, South Australia, Queensland and Tasmania, and also, if Her Majesty is satisfied that the people of Western Australia have agreed thereto, of Western Australia, shall be united in a Federal Commonwealth under the name of the Commonwealth of Australia. But the Queen may, at any time after the proclamation, appoint a Governor-General for the Commonwealth.

The Commonwealth shall be *were, made laws only for their particular colonies. A*

4. established, and the Constitution of the Commonwealth shall take effect, on and after the day so appointed. But the Parliaments of the several colonies may at any time after the passing of this Act make any such laws, to come into operation on the day so appointed, as they might have made of the Constitution had taken effect at the passing of this Act.
5. This Act, and all laws made by the Parliament of the Commonwealth under the Constitution, shall be binding on the courts, judges, and people of every State and of every part of the Commonwealth, notwithstanding anything in the laws of any State; and the laws of the Commonwealth shall be in force on all British ships, the Queen's ships of war excepted, whose first port of clearance and whose port of destination are in the Commonwealth.
6. "The Commonwealth" shall mean the Commonwealth of Australia as established under this Act.

"The States" shall mean such of the colonies of New South Wales, New Zealand, Queensland, Tasmania, Victoria, Western Australia, and South Australia, including the northern territory of South Australia, as for the time being are parts of the Commonwealth, and such colonies or territories as may be admitted into or established by the Commonwealth as States; and each of such parts of the Commonwealth shall be called "a State".

"Original States" shall mean such States as are parts of the Commonwealth at its establishment.

7. The Federal Council of Australasia Act, 1885, is hereby repealed, but so as not to affect any laws passed by the Federal Council of Australasia and in force at the establishment of the Commonwealth.

Any such law may be repealed as to any State by the Parliament of the Commonwealth, or as to any colony not being a State by the Parliament thereof.

8. After the passing of this Act the Colonial Boundaries Act, 1895, shall not apply to any colony which becomes a State of the Commonwealth; but the Commonwealth shall be taken to be a self-governing colony for the purposes of that Act.
9. The Constitution of the Commonwealth shall be as follows:-

## The Parliament – General Sections 1-6

### Section 1- Legislative Power

The legislative power of the Commonwealth shall be vested in a Federal Parliament, which shall consist of the Queen, a Senate, and a House of Representatives, and which is herein-after called "The Parliament," or "The Parliament of the Commonwealth."

**Section 2 – Governor-General**

A Governor-General appointed by the Queen shall be Her Majesty's representative in the Commonwealth, and shall have and may exercise in the Commonwealth during the Queen's pleasure, but subject to this Constitution, such powers and functions of the Queen as Her Majesty may be pleased to assign to him

**Section 3 – Salary of Governor-General**

There shall be payable to the Queen out of the Consolidated Revenue fund of the Commonwealth, for the salary of the Governor-General, an annual sum which, until the Parliament otherwise provides, shall be ten thousand pounds.

The salary of the Governor-General shall not be altered during his continuance in office.

This is only a tiny part of Australia's constitution.

The full constitution can be found at

http://australianpolitics.com/constitution-aus/text

# SO WHAT NOW?

# Chapter 13      SO WHAT NOW?

We Australians need to accept that Australia became a republic in 1986.

Australian citizens need to put together an independent body to rewrite the Australian constitution, in line with being a republic. We need changes that suit the Australian culture, and to evolve peacefully and harmoniously into the 21st century and beyond.

Do we ask the politicians to organise the rewrite of the constitution? No. That would be like asking an individual or union to write work-salary and benefits conditions. The corporation having to put up with whatever the workers demanded with no restrictions.

We must remember that the politicians and the judiciary are just public servants. They are employees of the citizens of the country.

These senior public servants (politicians and the judiciary), like all of us, want what is best for themselves personally. Politicians and Judges are using the citizens' money (taxes etc.) for their incomes and benefits. These come from the same purse that is paying pensions and welfare, emergency services, education, and hospitals etc.. And they need to be assessed appropriately; proportionally with all other incomes that come from the public purse. Pay rises, superannuation and benefits should be proportional to other government salaries and pensions.

The power of these senior public servants needs to have
- Standards, boundaries and limitations, set by the citizens of the country.
- The constitution needs to define the extent of the power of these public servants.

So the constitution needs to written by a non-political group of citizens not involved in politics or the judiciary.

There is no reason why such a body cannot be funded out of the public purse. This would give both validity and strength to a rewrite. When complete, changes could be ratified by the citizens, through a referendum.

A question: the rewrite and referendum, should this be done in part or whole? That is can we start with the foundation sections and then once the basis is agreed on, get the specifics done? The foundation sections of the constitution being:

1. ***Preamble, history and status of the nation***
   It is necessary to recognise as starting point, the time and culture of the nation. In doing so it is important to clearly summarize the relevant history of the nation to this point in time. Plus include the reasons for a need to update the constitution.

2. ***Long term Goals of the nation***
   To operate effectively, a democratic country needs to be clear in its long term goals, so that the focus is based on the long term not the short term election cycle. For this reason I have suggested we need to make long term goals to work toward. Clearly defining the sort of nation we want in the next hundred, two hundred years or more?

3. ***Humanitarian standards by which all laws and judgements need to meet***
   Everyone has their own values by which they see the world. Individual values may conflict with the values of the majority of citizens. Therefore the definition of the nation's humane standards and long term goals is vital. This will ensure the parliament and the judiciary systems are working with the same values'.

4. **A)** ***Conscious vote is to be the norm***. All politicians must vote for what's best for their constituents. In accordance with that, any-voted-in member cannot be forced to vote along any party or alliance lines. Forcing politicians to vote in any way other than conscience voting is illegal.
   **B)** ***Structure of the government***

5. Clearly state the ***Necessity of Accountability and Transparency*** in governance. For this I have suggested, that
   a) The objective for each section and subsection of the constitution is defined and written in the constitution.
   b) KPIs are implemented for all laws so their effectiveness can be evaluated; and if these laws not achieving the KPIs can be modified or deleted.

c) Open quarterly publication of expenditure of all government departments so the citizens can understand where their money is being spent.

So, where to now?

As mentioned above, the constitution needs to written by a non-political group of citizens, not employed in politics or the judiciary. This will need a citizen movement to initiate this important and necessary project.

Perhaps two stages are required
1) Principles defined and accepted in a referendum.
2) Once principles agreed and ratified, only then working details of governance can be written to complete the constitution.

I am willing to be a coordinator for such a project. So I need people with varying expertise to work as a team to get such a project going. This constitutional project requires a broad spectrum of people to work together with one purpose.  So email me: aflaweddemocracy@gmail.com

I want like-minded people with the **goal to "improve and strengthen democracy"** and specifically those who want to help rewrite Australia's constitution.

I don't want like-minded people who agree with all I have said in this book because there may be better ideas than I have presented here. Not all the ideas I have put forward in this book are ones I necessary hold but have been put here to get you thinking, analysing and debating.

If you think you can help in any way, please get in touch with me at

aflaweddemocracy@gmail.com

I look forward to a great constructive team to work with and to be part of.

JA Ehrlich

# APPENDIX

## Contents:
1) **United Nations Declaration of Human Rights**
2) **United Nations  The Human Rights of a Child**

*THE GENERAL ASSEMBLY proclaims THIS UNIVERSAL DECLARATION OF HUMAN RIGHTS as a common standard of achievement for all peoples and all nations, to the end that every individual and every organ of society, keeping this Declaration constantly in mind, shall strive by teaching and education to promote respect for these rights and freedoms and by progressive measures, national and international, to secure their universal and effective recognition and observance, both among the peoples of Member States themselves and among the peoples of territories under their jurisdiction.*

**Article 1.**

*All human beings are born free and equal in dignity and rights. They are endowed with reason and conscience and should act towards one another in a spirit of brotherhood.*

**Article 2.**

*Everyone is entitled to all the rights and freedoms set forth in this Declaration, without distinction of any kind, such as race, colour, sex, language, religion, political or other opinion, national or social origin, property, birth or other status. Furthermore, no distinction shall be made on the basis of the political, jurisdictional or international status of the country or territory to which a person belongs, whether it be independent, trust, non-self-governing or under any other limitation of sovereignty.*

**Article 3.**

*Everyone has the right to life, liberty and security of person.*

**Article 4.**

*No one shall be held in slavery or servitude; slavery and the slave trade shall be prohibited in all their forms.*

**Article 5.**

*No one shall be subjected to torture or to cruel, inhuman or degrading treatment or punishment.*

**Article 6.**

*Everyone has the right to recognition everywhere as a person before the law.*

**Article 7.**

*All are equal before the law and are entitled without any discrimination to equal protection of the law. All are entitled to equal protection against any discrimination in violation of this Declaration and against any incitement to such discrimination.*

**Article 8.**

*Everyone has the right to an effective remedy by the competent national tribunals for acts violating the fundamental rights granted him by the constitution or by law.*

**Article 9.**

*No one shall be subjected to arbitrary arrest, detention or exile.*

*Article 10.*

Everyone is entitled in full equality to a fair and public hearing by an independent and impartial tribunal, in the determination of his rights and obligations and of any criminal charge against him.

*Article 11.*

(1) Everyone charged with a penal offence has the right to be presumed innocent until proved guilty according to law in a public trial at which he has had all the guarantees necessary for his defence.

(2) No one shall be held guilty of any penal offence on account of any act or omission which did not constitute a penal offence, under national or international law, at the time when it was committed. Nor shall a heavier penalty be imposed than the one that was applicable at the time the penal offence was committed.

*Article 12.*

No one shall be subjected to arbitrary interference with his privacy, family, home or correspondence, nor to attacks upon his honour and reputation. Everyone has the right to the protection of the law against such interference or attacks.

*Article 13.*

(1) Everyone has the right to freedom of movement and residence within the borders of each state.

(2) Everyone has the right to leave any country, including his own, and to return to his country.

*Article 14.*

(1) Everyone has the right to seek and to enjoy in other countries asylum from persecution.

(2) This right may not be invoked in the case of prosecutions genuinely arising from non-political crimes or from acts contrary to the purposes and principles of the United Nations.

*Article 15.*

(1) Everyone has the right to a nationality.

(2) No one shall be arbitrarily deprived of his nationality nor denied the right to change his nationality.

*Article 16.*

(1) Men and women of full age, without any limitation due to race, nationality or religion, have the right to marry and to found a family. They are entitled to equal rights as to marriage, during marriage and at its dissolution.

(2) Marriage shall be entered into only with the free and full consent of the intending spouses.

(3) The family is the natural and fundamental group unit of society and is entitled to protection by society and the State.

*Article 17.*

(1) Everyone has the right to own property alone as well as in association with others.

(2) No one shall be arbitrarily deprived of his property.

*Article 18.*

Everyone has the right to freedom of thought, conscience and religion; this right includes freedom to change his religion or belief, and freedom, either alone or in community with others and in public or private, to manifest his religion or belief in teaching, practice, worship and observance.

**Article 19.**

Everyone has the right to freedom of opinion and expression; this right includes freedom to hold opinions without interference and to seek, receive and impart information and ideas through any media and regardless of frontiers.

**Article 20.**

(1) Everyone has the right to freedom of peaceful assembly and association.

(2) No one may be compelled to belong to an association.[23]

**Article 21.**

(1) Everyone has the right to take part in the government of his country, directly or through freely chosen representatives.

(2) Everyone has the right of equal access to public service in his country.

(3) The will of the people shall be the basis of the authority of government; this will shall be expressed in periodic and genuine elections which shall be by universal and equal suffrage and shall be held by secret vote or by equivalent free voting procedures.

**Article 22.**

Everyone, as a member of society, has the right to social security and is entitled to realization, through national effort and international co-operation and in accordance with the organization and resources of each State, of the economic, social and cultural rights indispensable for his dignity and the free development of his personality.

**Article 23.**

(1) Everyone has the right to work, to free choice of employment, to just and favourable conditions of work and to protection against unemployment.

(2) Everyone, without any discrimination, has the right to equal pay for equal work.

(3) Everyone who works has the right to just and favourable remuneration ensuring for himself and his family an existence worthy of human dignity, and supplemented, if necessary, by other means of social protection.

(4) Everyone has the right to form and to join trade unions for the protection of his interests.

**Article 24.**

Everyone has the right to rest and leisure, including reasonable limitation of working hours and periodic holidays with pay.

**Article 25.**

(1) Everyone has the right to a standard of living adequate for the health and well-being of himself and of his family, including food, clothing, housing and medical care and necessary social services, and the right to security in the event of unemployment, sickness, disability, widowhood, old age or other lack of livelihood in circumstances beyond his control.

(2) Motherhood and childhood are entitled to special care and assistance. All children, whether born in or out of wedlock, shall enjoy the same social protection.

---

[23] http://www.un.org/en/documents/udhr/ accessed on 28 October 2013

*Article 26.*

*(1) Everyone has the right to education. Education shall be free, at least in the elementary and fundamental stages. Elementary education shall be compulsory. Technical and professional education shall be made generally available and higher education shall be equally accessible to all on the basis of merit.*

*(2) Education shall be directed to the full development of the human personality and to the strengthening of respect for human rights and fundamental freedoms. It shall promote understanding, tolerance and friendship among all nations, racial or religious groups, and shall further the activities of the United Nations for the maintenance of peace.*

*(3) Parents have a prior right to choose the kind of education that shall be given to their children.*

*Article 27.*

*(1) Everyone has the right freely to participate in the cultural life of the community, to enjoy the arts and to share in scientific advancement and its benefits.*

*(2) Everyone has the right to the protection of the moral and material interests resulting from any scientific, literary or artistic production of which he is the author.*

*Article 28.*

*Everyone is entitled to a social and international order in which the rights and freedoms set forth in this Declaration can be fully realized.*

*Article 29.*

*(1) Everyone has duties to the community in which alone the free and full development of his personality is possible.*

*(2) In the exercise of his rights and freedoms, everyone shall be subject only to such limitations as are determined by law solely for the purpose of securing due recognition and respect for the rights and freedoms of others and of meeting the just requirements of morality, public order and the general welfare in a democratic society.*

- *(3) These rights and freedoms may in no case be exercised contrary to the purposes and principles of the United Nations.*

*Article 30.*

- *Nothing in this Declaration may be interpreted as implying for any State, group or person any right to engage in any activity or to perform any act aimed at the destruction of any of the rights and freedoms set forth herein.*

## Children's Rights

On top of the rights of an individual are the rights of a child. In view of Australia's dismal history in regard to children, I think this is vital. Here I am not just referring to The Stolen Generation of the aboriginal, but also the Orange children, the forced adoptions, the ignorance of paedophilia and currently refugee children in detention.

**DECLARATION OF THE HUMAN RIGHTS OF A CHILD** *10 December 1959*[24]

*WHEREAS the peoples of the United Nations have, in the Charter, reaffirmed their faith in fundamental human rights and in the dignity and worth of the human person, and have determined to promote social progress and better standards of life in larger freedom,*

*WHEREAS the United Nations has, in the Universal Declaration of Human Rights, proclaimed that everyone is entitled to all the rights and freedoms set forth therein, without distinction of any kind, such as race, colour, sex, language, religion, political or other opinion, national or social origin, property, birth or other status,*

*WHEREAS the child, by reason of his physical and mental immaturity, needs special safeguards and care, including appropriate legal protection, before as well as after birth,*

*WHEREAS the need for such special safeguards has been stated in the Geneva Declaration of the Rights of the Child of 1924, and recognized in the Universal Declaration of Human Rights and in the statutes of specialized agencies and international organizations concerned with the welfare of children,*

*WHEREAS mankind owes to the child the best it has to give,*

*The General Assembly*

*Now, therefore,*                                          *Proclaims*

*THIS DECLARATION OF THE RIGHTS OF THE CHILD to the end that he may have a happy childhood and enjoy for his own good and for the good of society the rights and freedoms herein set forth, and calls upon parents, upon men and women as individuals, and upon voluntary organizations, local authorities and national Governments to recognize these rights and strive for their observance by legislative and other measures progressively taken in accordance with the following principles:*

1    *The child shall enjoy all the rights set forth in this Declaration. Every child, without any exception whatsoever, shall be entitled to these rights, without distinction or discrimination on account of race, colour, sex, language, religion, political or other opinion, national or social origin, property, birth or other status, whether of himself or of his family.*

2    *The child shall enjoy special protection, and shall be given opportunities and facilities, by law and by other means, to enable him to develop physically, mentally, morally, spiritually and socially in a healthy and normal manner and in conditions of freedom and dignity. In the enactment of laws for this purpose, the best interests of the child shall be the paramount consideration.*

3    *The child shall be entitled from his birth to a name and a nationality.*

4    *The child shall enjoy the benefits of social security. He shall be entitled to grow and develop in health; to this end, special care and protection shall be provided both to him and to his mother, including adequate pre-natal and post-natal care. The child shall have the right to adequate nutrition, housing, recreation and medical services.*

5    *The child who is physically, mentally or socially handicapped shall be given the special*

---

[24] http://www.un.org/cyberschoolbus/humanrights/resources/child.asp    28 October 2013

*treatment, education and care required by his particular condition.*

6    *The child, for the full and harmonious development of his personality, needs love and understanding. He shall, wherever possible, grow up in the care and under the responsibility of his parents, and, in any case, in an atmosphere of affection and of moral and material security; a child of tender years shall not, save in exceptional circumstances, be separated from his mother. Society and the public authorities shall have the duty to extend particular care to children without a family and to those without adequate means of support. Payment of State and other assistance towards the maintenance of children of large families is desirable.*

# Other books by this author

## A Lioness from Judea Roars
### A Lioness from Judea Cries

## A Pale Blue Suitcase
### Divorce Pathways

JA Ehrlich wrote her first book, an autobiography,
*A Lioness from Judea Roars –A Lioness from Judea Cries*
for cathartic reasons, and then was encouraged to publish it. She has never promoted this book as she didn't feel she wanted to dwell in the past.

The second book *A Pale Blue Suitcase* came about due to that rhetoric dinner party question following her first book "Well how would you change the system?"
She suggests that this question is a quick way to end a dinner party so read the book instead. It is an excellent, easy to read and thorough insight into positive change.

www.ingramcontent.com/pod-product-compliance
Lightning Source LLC
Chambersburg PA
CBHW052009280526
45793CB00005B/913